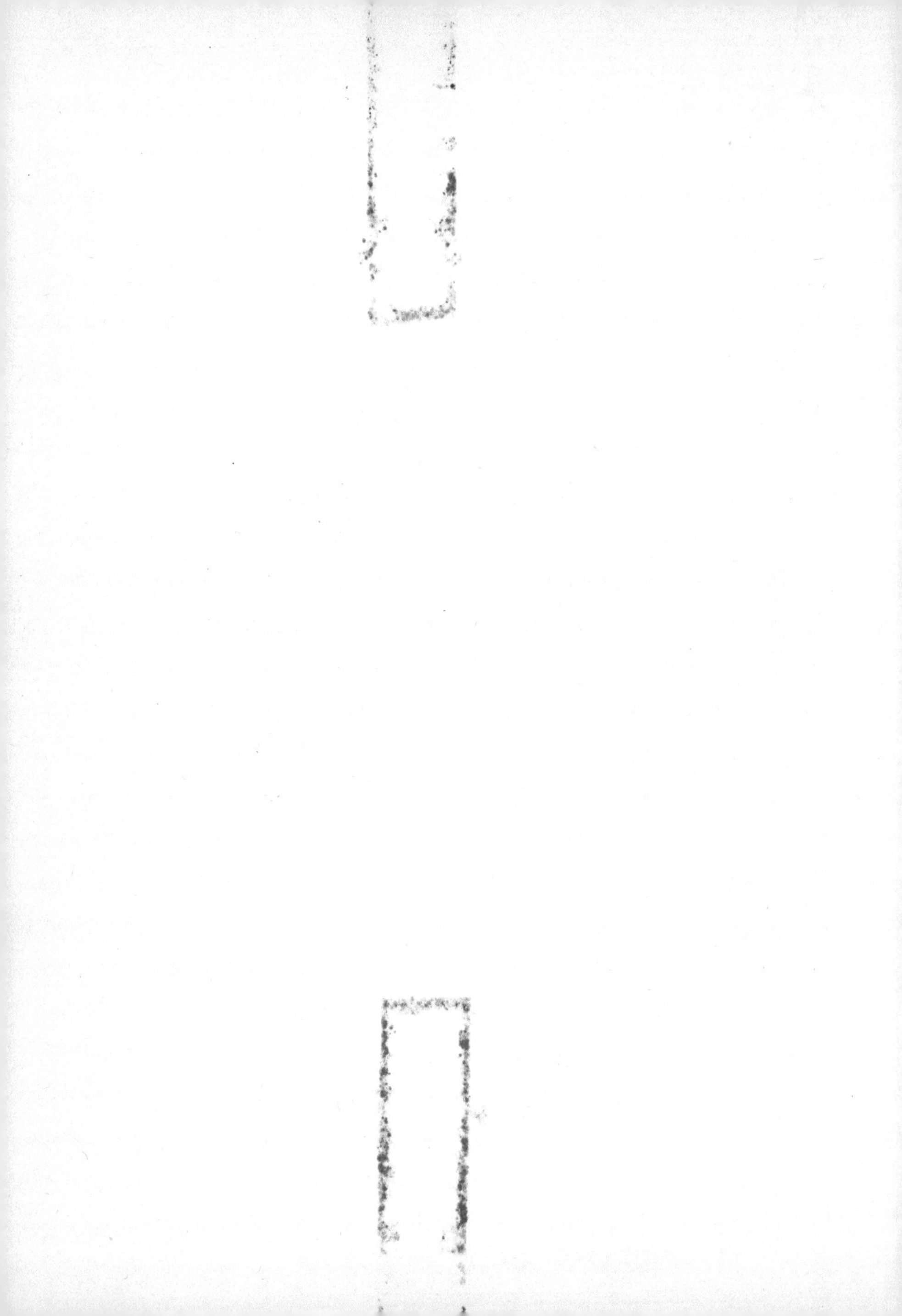

GEORGE WASHIN

BY GENEVIEVE

GTON

FOSTER

CHARLES SCRIBNER'S SONS - NEW YORK

PRINTED IN THE UNITED STATES OF AMERICA

J-4.67(AJ)

For
Charles Cole
and his father,
John

born 1732

THE FAMILY

THE YEAR was 1732. It was a February morning, on a tobacco plantation in the King of England's oldest colony, Virginia. And it was almost ten o'clock. In the living room of a small, low house overlooking the Potomac River, Mr. Augustine Washington waited impatiently, pacing slowly back and forth before a closed door opposite the fireplace.

Occasionally he pulled from his waistcoat pocket a chunky, gold watch and compared its hands with those of the grandfather clock in the corner, which barely seemed to move. He walked to the window and stood looking out through its small, square panes into the fresh spring morning, his legs in their cream colored stockings wide apart, his hands folded beneath the tails of his purple coat.

Suddenly, with a click of the latch, the door behind him opened. There, at last, stood an old Negro woman with a small white bundle in her arms.

"Here he be, Marse Washington. A boy. A mighty fine, big boy" she said, her shining brown face wrinkled into a broad smile, as she proudly held the newborn son for his father to see.

"Let's call him GEORGE" said his mother later, when they were choosing a name for him. He was Mary Ball Washington's first son, and she wished him to be named for the man who had been her guardian.

"GEORGE!" exclaimed her husband.

George WASHINGTON? George was the name of their King, to be sure,–the King of England. But who ever heard of a Washington by the name of George?

Augustine and Lawrence, now, were regular family names, and so was John. It was his grandfather John, who had been the first Washington to leave England. Sixty six years ago, he had come to Virginia to raise tobacco on this very plantation, here on the *Potomac River.*

But Mary Ball Washington was very positive, and Augustine was agreeable. So, in April, when he was baptized, their baby son, born on the 22nd of February 1732, was given the name he would make famous.

Little George Washington was just learning to walk, not yet steady on his feet when a baby sister was born. They called her Betty. She had the same gray blue eyes as her brother, sandy light brown hair, and soon looked almost like his twin.

The next year, small brother Sam was rocking in the cradle. And when George was past six, and could count to ten and ride his pony all over the plantation, he had three little brothers Sam, John, and Charlie.

Then it was that father Washington told his family they were going to move. He had bought a new plantation. It was called Ferry Farm, he said, and was on another river, named the Rappahannock.

They had moved once before, but George could not remember it. But this move was exciting—to see everything packed up—to ride in the coach all day from early morning, through the woods over the bumpy roads, then finally to see the house with the sun setting behind it. It was a dark red house, standing among some pine trees on a hill.

Inside were eight rooms. George and Betty ran in and out counting them, upstairs and down, opening all the doors, peering in the closets, watching the baggage carried in, seeing the beds being made up, and finding out where everyone was going to sleep.

Next morning early they were out exploring the grounds, looking into the dairy house, the store houses, the kitchen, all the other small separate buildings, the stables and the well. Then they ran down the hill to see the river and the Ferry Boat.

The river was disappointing. It looked so narrow compared to the Potomac, but the Ferry Boat was thrilling. It started right at their own wharf, and carried people and horses across the river to the town of Fredericksburg.

Aunt Mildred lived in Fredericksburg. Until they went over to visit her, George had never in all his life, been in a town. And there was so much to see! Houses and shops stood close together. Down by the wharf on the river, there were long tobacco warehouses. There was a county courthouse, a prison made of stone, and a church with a steeple.

Reverend Mr. Marye was the preacher, and he also had a school. At noon his boys were out playing in the yard. And later, five or six of them were in the apothecary's shop, buying brown sugar candy.

George wished very much to be one of them. He was almost seven. Mr. Hobby had taught him to count. Why couldn't he go to school with the boys in Fredericksburg and ride over on the Ferry every day?

THE TOBACCO SHIP

THE MINUTE he opened his eyes one April morning, George was out of bed. It was earlier than usual, but he hurried into his shirt, jumped into his brown trousers and tied the shirr string in the back, as fast as possible. He didn't want to waste a minute.

This was the day the ship was to be loaded. A big ship had come from England a few days before, filled with splendid things for all the family—new shoes and hats, and toys and tools and dishes—all kinds of fine things, that were made in England. Now it was being loaded with tobacco for the voyage back.

Calling to Betty and Sam as he ran by, George sped down the stairs, out onto the wet grass and along the path of soft pine needles toward the river. At the end of the wharf, he could see the ship, with its three tall masts. Half way down were the men—his father and the Captain, the overseer of the plantation and ten or twelve Negroes, handling the barrels.

"Hi thar, boy! Already? Let 'er go!" shouted the men as they sent one huge barrel after another rolling down the slope, thumping along the wharf, over gang plank and into the ship's hold.

George climbed up on one of the barrels where he would be out of the way, but could see everything.

Just then there came a cry. A rope had slipped. A barrel had gone wild and was careening down the slope, headed for the water. The men on the pier caught it just in time. To lose a barrel in that careless way would have been most unfortunate, because tobacco was used for money in Virginia.

Exactly how many things one barrel of tobacco would buy in England, George didn't know, but never enough, his father seemed to think. He was talking to the Captain about it later, when they were having a second breakfast, this time with the family.

So far, George had quite forgotten to be hungry but now he had room for fish cakes, and bacon, four or five pieces of corn bread, besides three mugs of milk. And he had one more waffle, each time the cook's small boy came running in with fresh ones, hot and crisp from the kitchen.

"It's discouraging" his father was saying to the Captain "each year we get less and less for our tobacco. The merchants in London are allowed to set the price, so what can we do about it?"

The Captain shook his head and vowed it was a problem. He told how hard it was to keep tobacco dry at sea, and also spoke about the voyage. If they had good wind and weather, he dared say they'd be back across the Atlantic in three weeks.

George listened to every word the Captain had to say. It must be a fine life, he thought to be the captain of a tobacco ship. Some day he would like to wear a bright blue uniform with silver buttons, and go sailing back and forth to England on important voyages!

BIG BROTHER LAWRENCE

"HALT! Shoulder arms! For-wa-a-ard- MARCH!" Back and forth and around a vacant lot in Fredericksburg, marched a company of soldiers, drilling, getting ready for war. School was out. Reverend Marye had dismissed his boys and a knot of eight or nine year olds, George among them, stood by watching, singling out their friends and relatives.

"There he is—George! The Captain!" shouted one of them. "There's your big brother, Lawrence!"

Captain Lawrence Washington! George had already seen him. His heart was thumping so hard inside his shirt, he was afraid the boys would see it, and blame him for being too proud of having such

Sold to
Tobacco
FERRY FAR

1

a wonderful big brother,–captain of the company.

It was not long that George had known this big brother of his, only since Lawrence had come home from England. But all his life he had heard of Lawrence and of Augustine, or "Austin" as he was called. They were his two half-brothers.

Almost as soon as George was born, Lawrence, who was then fourteen, and Austin, who was twelve, had been sent to school in England. It was the same school to which their father had gone, when he was a boy and where George would be going, when he was old enough. Austin was still there, but Lawrence had come home. He was twenty-three now, and captain of this company forming in Fredericksburg.

And he was going to war. England was at war with Spain, Lawrence had explained to George. They were fighting on this side of the ocean down in the West Indies. An English Admiral, by the name of Vernon, had already captured one of the Spanish forts. The King had asked the Colonies in America to send a number of soldiers. So Lawrence had enlisted.

The first night he came home with his new sword, he let George touch the beautiful, shining blade and even try on the coat of his new uniform, being careful not to step backward on the tails.

A few weeks later, to the sound of fife and drum, clanking swords and cheering people, George saw Lawrence and his company march aboard their ship and sail away. The town seemed dull and empty to the little boys, until one of them had a bright idea. Off they all ran to the vacant lot, to march about like soldiers, making believe they had real guns and swords instead of sticks and cornstalks. Two years passed before the war was over and the soldiers returned. By that time, George had grown at least six inches taller, could run faster, ride better, and throw a stone farther than almost any other ten-year-old.

And Austin was home. He had come home, bringing something to everyone from England, letters and newspapers to his father, tea for his stepmother, a toy or book for his little brothers and sister. George loved Austin, he was so kind and friendly. Still he could not take the place of Lawrence. George could hardly wait for Lawrence to come home.

And one day he was there! And then what tales he had to tell—all about the campaign and the commander, Admiral Vernon, who was so brave and skillful. Lawrence was dark and handsome. His eyes shone as he talked, and his slim hands moved in quick, easy gestures. On a low bench, facing him, George watched and listened, spellbound. There was nobody,—nobody so wonderful as his brother Lawrence!

George's mother didn't think so. She was partial to her own son. He looked sturdier, less spindly, and more like her own kindred, the Balls.

Their father loved all of his children equally but, like any Englishman, it was quite natural for Mr. Washington to take special interest in his eldest son who would some day be head of the family.

George was only eleven when his father died. It happened very suddenly, in April. The fields were green with new tobacco. George was away visiting some cousins, when a messenger came to bring him home at once. His father was very ill.

He tiptoed into the darkened room, and there he lay, the big man, stretched out on his bed, looking strange and unnaturally white.

Soon he was gone, and George's mother was weeping. Then came the funeral, with all the boys wearing their best suits, and Betty's hair tied with a black ribbon. Then came the reading of the will, which said that his father, according to custom had left most of what he owned to his eldest son, Lawrence. When it was all over, George saw his mother's face was solemn and set.

"Things are going to be very different for us now," she told him in a gloomy voice. "How we'll ever manage to get along, I certainly don't know. My poor, poor boy, you won't be able to do what you would have done, if your dear father had lived."

That meant that he could never go to school in England, George knew that. But surely, it didn't mean that they wouldn't have enough to eat and wear! It couldn't. Not so long as they had Ferry Farm. And wasn't that what the will said—that Ferry Farm was to be his when he was twenty-one?

His mother nodded.

Well, then, she could keep on living there, as long as she wanted to. By the time he was grown up, he would buy more plantations and be a wealthy man!

His mother kept on shaking her head. Where would he get the money to buy them? she asked dismally.

George didn't know exactly, but he was sure that he would find a way to earn it, somehow.

Then he would buy acres and acres of land, and ship barrels and barrels of tobacco to England, every year, and get all the things they wanted.

GOOD MANNERS

PROPPED up in front of George, one winter day, between a pewter inkwell and a jar of sand for blotting was a faded, green book. George was preparing to copy it. He took a bite of an apple. Then he dipped his goose quill, and on the first sheet of his copy book, carefully wrote this title:

Rules of Civility & Decent Behaviour
In Company and Converſation

That was just what he wanted, he thought. Next time he went to visit Lawrence, he would know exactly how to act—just as well perhaps, as if he had gone to school in England.

George was now past thirteen. Both of his older brothers were married and he often went to visit them, sometimes staying several months. Often he was away so long, that Betty and his little brothers thought he must have gone away to live. But he always came back—his mother saw to that.

Austin was now living on the plantation, in the very house, where George was born. Lawrence had taken for his home a plantation farther up the Potomac River, where the family had lived from the time George was three, until they moved to Ferry Farm. The old house had burned down, so Lawrence had built a new one, and in honor of Admiral Vernon, he had named it MOUNT VERNON.

Visiting Lawrence and Anne at Mount Vernon was quite different from living with Jane and Austin at Wakefield. There it was comfortable and pleasant, but very much like home. Going to Mount Vernon was like entering another world.

At Mount Vernon, life was elegant, and fashionable and exciting. Important people were always coming and going—officers in the navy, and the British army—friends of Lawrence's from England as well as the finest gentlemen of the colony. There were big dinners, card games in the evening, and fox hunting in the early mornings.

And there was Anne's family, who lived on the neighboring plantation. Sir William Fairfax, her father, was a most splendid gentleman—truly a nobleman. His cousin who lived in England was a Lord and was enormously rich. Lawrence said that he owned more than 5,000,000 acres of land here in Virginia, beyond the Blue Ridge Mountains.

Land. That was what they talked most about, Lawrence and Sir William, about schemes for buying more land and adding more plantations to the ones they owned. And that was what George wanted to do.

That was the way he planned to live, someday, just the way Lawrence lived at Mount Vernon. Only one thing worried him. Everyone at Mount Vernon had such perfect manners. They always knew just the right thing to do, without seeming to think about it. And he didn't. Sometimes he wasn't sure whether to sit down or stand up, whether to shake hands or just bow or what to do with his hands and feet or where to put them. That was why he had been so glad to find this book of rules. The first one had caught his eye. Then he read snatches here and there:

"Every action done in Company, (he read) ought to be with Some Sign of Respect to those that are Present . . . If you cough, Sneeze, Sigh or Yawn, do it not Loud, but privately . . . Sleep not when others speak, Sit not when others stand . . . Spit not in the fire . . . In Pulling off your Hat to persons of Distinction . . . If any one come to Speak to you while you are Sitting Stand up. . . . Shew not yourself glad at the Misfortune of another though he were your enemy . . . Cleanse not your teeth with the Table Cloth," . . . and so on . . .

Wasn't that just what he wanted? Rules to go by. And 110 of them! He would copy them all!

So that was what he was starting upon, with the book propped up in front of him. Fortified with several apples, a handful of walnuts and a chunk of brown sugar, he had now sharpened his quill to a fine point and written the title.

He copied as many pages as he could that day, and more the next, and kept on until he had come at last to number 110.

"Labour to keep alive in your Breast that Little Spark of Celstial Fire called Conscience."

He misspelled "celestial" but he finished off with a fine flourish of scrolls and the Latin word

Finis

Meaning THE END!

He had the rules. Now all he had to do was to practice them! and make Lawrence proud of him.

THE SEA OR SURVEYING?

SURVEYORS were at work one day, on the vacant lot in Fredericksburg, where the soldiers used to drill. They were laying out a new street, dragging chains, moving rods, squinting across their three legged compasses and waving their arms.

Standing by to watch were a group of boys, George among them. Big boys they were now, fourteen years old or more, all wishing they might be allowed to help. As it happened, one of the rod men left early, and George saw a chance to take his place. Then, as he helped gather up the chain, he asked how much men were paid for helping surveyors. That gave him an idea. And he remembered something!

He ran for the ferry, but it was gone. Having to wait threw him into a rage of impatience. It would be too dark now, at home. His mother wouldn't allow a lighted candle in the storage closet.

But early next morning he was in there, rummaging about. Behind a broken spinning wheel, under an old chair with a torn red leather seat, he found what he was looking for, a big, brown wooden box with an iron handle, and a bundle of sticks strapped to it. Old surveying instruments, that had been his father's.

Out into the open space beyond the cabbage patch he carried them. Three curious, young brothers followed close behind. Unfolding the three legs, George stood them up, took out the compass, screwed it on where the legs met. It was perfect! He had the instruments! He would become a surveyor! It took Mathematics, but it was easy for him. And Mr. Williams, who lived near Austin, was a very good teacher. If he could get a job as a rod man, he could learn to draw plans and measure by watching the surveyors. He was sure Lawrence would think it was a sensible idea. Some day, after he had learned to do it well enough, Colonel Fairfax or Lawrence might ask him to measure out a new plantation.

But, before talking with his brother, George had a letter from him, proposing a plan that sounded so much more exciting, that for weeks to come, he could think of nothing else but GOING TO SEA!

That was it.

"How would you like to go to sea" Lawrence had said—be an officer in the navy? Friends of his, he thought, would help to get George an appointment.

Go to sea? Be an officer in the British navy? Rushing through George's mind went all that Lawrence had ever told him about Admiral Vernon. Would it be possible for him to start as a midshipman and work up to be an admiral? ADMIRAL WASHINGTON, he thought, seeing himself in a dazzling gold braided uniform with a high white plume waving in his hat.

Then he came down to earth. He was only fourteen, he couldn't go to sea at all, unless his mother gave her consent. Lawrence said in his letter that he feared she wouldn't. And she didn't. She said positively no. Have her dear boy go to sea? Out on that terrible dangerous ocean? She wouldn't hear of it. The most she could be persuaded to do was to write her brother Joseph in England, for his opinion. And she was well satisfied with Uncle Joseph's reply, when, after many weeks, it came. This is part of what he wrote:

My dear Sister:

I understand that you have some thought of putting your son George to sea. I think he had better be put as apprentice to a tinker, than be a common sailor before the mast. For they will cut and slash and use him like a dog. As to any preferment in the navy, it is not to be expected. And if he should get to be the master of a Virginia ship, a planter that has three or four hundred acres and three or four slaves may live more comfortably. I pray God keep you and yours.

Your loving brother,

Joseph Ball.

George was not surprised. He had half expected it. And he was not half so disappointed as he might have been, if the letter had not been so long in coming. While waiting, he had gone on with his surveying. Soon he was to forget all about what he couldn't do in the thrill of what he could do.

Just three months later, he was allowed to make a survey all by himself—his first one. Under the figures in his field book, he wrote the date, August 18, 1747. He was fifteen and a half.

Not so long after that came the great day, when he was paid for a survey in real money. Going home at night with two pounds five shillings in his pocket made him feel like a man,—really and truly a surveyor.

Now in this fall, when George was fifteen, he left Ferry Farm. Taking his surveying instruments, his copy book, and a new razor (which he didn't quite need) he went to live with Lawrence at Mount Vernon.

There he learned that Lord Fairfax, the man he was most curious to see—the man who owned 5,000,000 acres of land,—had just arrived from England.

A NEW FRIEND, LORD FAIRFAX

LORD Thomas Fairfax took an instant liking to Lawrence Washington's young brother. And George was very much impressed by His Lordship, though he was amazed, at first, to find him so much gruffer and more short spoken than his cousin, Sir William.

And he had no use for the ladies—none at all. He sat in a remote corner of the next room, pretending to read through one entire party.

It was a starry winter night, during the Christmas holidays. The Fairfax's wide entrance hall, hung with evergreen and bright with many candles, had been cleared for dancing. As the spinet and the fiddle sounded the opening notes of the minuet, men in gay satin coats bowed low before the ladies of their choice. George stood in the doorway watching them.

Lawrence and Anne were first upon the floor, followed by Anne's brother, George Fairfax, and his bride-to-be, the lovely Sally Carey. Sally, in a pink gown, with a rose in her brown hair, was the most enchanting, bewitching young lady George had ever seen. He hesitated, wishing, not daring, then at last mustering up courage to ask her younger sister to dance. Then he wished he hadn't. She reminded him too much of his "Lowland Beauty," a girl at home who had broken his heart. Too late to retreat, he held her hand high, and kept his mind on his dancing.

"A very well mannered lad, young George" observed Sir William, stopping for a word with Lord Fairfax. "Too bad he's so bashful with the girls."

"Not at all. Not at all" snapped his gaunt old cousin "It will keep him out of grief."

Lord Fairfax spoke with feeling. He had come to America, on purpose, it was said, to forget a lovely lady who had been cruel to him,–to bury himself in the wilderness with his books. On his land beyond the Blue Ridge Mountains, he was planning to build himself a home. He was stopping for just a short while with his cousin Sir William.

His instant liking for George increased as the months went by. He liked the way the boy rode a horse, and handled the dogs when they went hunting. He liked his grave straightforward way with older men. He liked the careful, exact way in which he practiced his surveying, measuring out a turnip patch for his brother with as much care as if he were laying out a highway for the King.

"How would it suit you to do some surveying for

THE WILDERNESS

me?" he asked one day, and before the delighted George could catch his breath, went on to explain.

The property which he owned, those 5,000,000 acres, was for the most part wild uncultivated forest which had never been surveyed—just Indian country. In order to sell off plantations, he must have the boundaries marked. So, in early March, he was planning to send out a party of surveyors.

There would be George Fairfax (Anne's brother, who was eight years older than George) another more experienced surveyor, and George, that is, he added dryly, if George would care to go.

Would he care to go! Wasn't that just the chance he had been hoping for? To measure and see that new land? To pick out a good piece to buy, when he had saved the money? He could hardly wait to start.

He decided to keep a Journal and write down everything he saw. He had a new notebook—almost empty. On the first pages were only a few love poems he had tried to write to his "Lowland Beauty" and two other cruel girls. They didn't matter now. His fifteen year old heart was already mended. He had something else to write and think about. His Journey over the Mountains—his first long surveying trip—his first adventure in the wilderness!

GEORGE'S JOURNAL

"FRYDAY the 11th of March 1748" was the day that George's Journal began. That morning, he and George Fairfax mounted their horses and started on their Journey. At first, on either side lay broad tobacco fields and blossoming cherry orchards, but as they rode west, fewer and fewer cultivated plantations broke into the deeper stretches of forest.

Next morning they were forty miles from home and met by the chief surveyor, Mr. Genn. All day they were climbing gradually, until late afternoon brought them out on the crest of the Blue Ridge Mountains. Below them spread the beautiful valley of the Shenandoah with the river winding through it, and on the far horizon rose the high, dark ridges of the Alleghanies. But George was not thinking about scenery. Tired and hungry, he was wondering how far it was down to the river and the nearby inn.

Next day, on their way up the river valley toward the hunting lodge of Lord Fairfax, George was marvelling at the maple sugar trees and the richness of the new land, wherever pioneers had cleared and planted their fields of grain and tobacco.

Tuesday was their first day spent in surveying. They were in the "Marshes" working hard all day. If he hadn't been so tired, George thought he would not have slept at all that night. It was the first one he ever spent in a pioneer's log cabin.

Not being so good a woodsmen as the others, he undressed as usual, he said, and "went to Bed, as they called it, when to my Surprize, I found it to be nothing but a little Straw Matted together without Sheets or anything else but one thread Bear blanket with double its weight of Lice and Fleas." Jumping up he put on his clothes in a hurry, and from then on, slept with the others on the floor, in front of the fireplace, rolled in his blanket.

On Friday, they had been gone a week, and had reached a branch of the Potomac River, which was so high with melted snow from the mountains that they had to swim the horses over to the Maryland side. There they plodded along toward an Indian trading post, over the worst road "ever trod by man or beast," blocked by fallen trees, overgrown with bushes, drenched with rain. It rained for three days.

Wednesday, about two o'clock, it cleared and they saw Indians coming from war, about thirty of them, but with only one scalp. Warmed by a drink of rum, the Indians were inspired to put on a war dance. "There manner of Dauncing is as follows" wrote George. "They clear a large Circle and make a Great Fire in the middle, then seat themselves around it. The best Dauncer Jumps up and Runs and Jumps about the Ring in a most comicle Manner followed by the rest. There Musick is a Pot of Water with a Deer-skin Stretched over it & a goard with some Shott in it to Rattle & a piece of an Horses Tail tied to it. One keeps Rattling, the other Drumming while the others are Dauncing." All day Thursday was spent watching and talking with these amazing red men.

The next two weeks were filled with constant surveying, 500 acres or more a day. Now they were sleeping in their tent and living on wild turkeys, which they shot and roasted over the open fire. One night while they slept, the straw on which they were lying caught on fire. On two or more nights their tent was blown away by a blustering wind.

Finally on Sunday, April 10th, they were ready to leave. Rolling up their tent, they turned their horses heads back again toward the Blue Ridge Mountains and, wrote George, "Wednesday the 13th of April 1748, Mr. Fairfax got safe home and I myself safe to my Brothers, which concludes my Journal."

LAWRENCE LEAVES MOUNT VERNON

A GAME of whist was being played one sultry summer afternoon, in a shady corner at Mount Vernon. It was Lawrence Washington's deal. Shuffling the cards, he dealt one each to Austin, to George, to George Fairfax. Then he laid down the pack, forced to admit that he did not feel well enough to play.

George was disappointed. He was learning the game fast, and nearly always had good luck. And not only at cards, but as a surveyor he was doing well.

All Spring, he had been helping to survey and lay out the new town of Alexandria, about eight miles up the Potomac River from Mount Vernon. Now, this day in July, his part in the work was finished. All was ready for the public sale of lots, which Austin and Lawrence were planning to attend the following day.

As he rose from the card table, Lawrence looked pale, but no one suspected how ill he was. Only thirty-one, he had but three more years to live.

During those three years, George was to go steadily forward. By fall, he had been sworn in as a public surveyor, and was surveying for Lord Fairfax again, beyond the Blue Ridge Mountains. Very well paid, he was saving his money for land, and by the following fall, when he was eighteen, he had enough to buy his first plantation—1000 acres! And he had 456 acres more by Christmas, when he went to see his mother and the boys at Ferry Farm, and Betty, who was now Mrs. Lewis, living in Fredericksburg.

At Mount Vernon, Lawrence was growing weaker. He thought that a trip to the West Indies might help him, but Anne could not go, because of their new baby girl. Would George be willing, he wondered, to miss several months of surveying? George would have done anything to see his brother well again.

They sailed directly from the Potomac, and after a month at sea, of which George kept a daily record, they landed on the green, tropical island of Barbados, rich in sugar cane and pineapples. Its sun and sea breeze, unfortunately, were of no benefit to Lawrence. And George came down with smallpox! He returned from that only sea voyage he was ever to take, his face scarred forever, with smallpox pits.

Lawrence came home, knowing that he had not long to live. He died in the summer of 1752. His will, when settled, made George heir to a large share of what his brother had owned, and also master of his beautiful plantation home, MOUNT VERNON.

A letter from the English Governor to the French Commander
FRENCH &

Une lettre
du
Commandant
français
au
Gouverneur
anglais
IDIAN WAR

THE FRENCH AND INDIAN WAR

YOUNG Major George Washington, now over six feet tall, and dressed in the blue uniform of a Virginia soldier, stood before the Governor, in his mansion or "Palace" at Williamsburg.

"How soon can you start?" asked the Governor, as he signed, sealed and handed George a letter.

"Today, sir" answered George. Soon he was out in the crisp October morning, far down the road on his galloping horse, leaving Williamsburg behind.

It was October 30, 1753. George was twenty-one years old. He was proud to be trusted with this difficult errand. He had asked for it. And he was determined to succeed,–though it meant following a dim, uncertain trail into the dangerous northwest.

The letter which he carried was to be delivered to the commander of a French fort somewhere near the Ohio River. The Governor could not say exactly where. He only knew that the French had come down from the north and were on land that belonged to the English–on the very land, in fact, which the King had given to the Ohio Company. For George, *that* had real meaning. His brother Lawrence had been President of that company of Virginians, when they received the land. Before Lawrence died, the Ohio Company had been planning to build a fort on their land, to protect it from the French. The fort had not been built. The French were there.

Now George was to carry the Governor's firm but courteous letter asking the French commander to leave. How many soldiers he had, how many forts the French had built, how many Indian tribes they had to help them—that, also, George was to find out.

As he rode along, he was thinking over what he needed—arms, ammunition, compasses, tents, food for the horses, presents for the Indians, as well as guides and interpreters. Stopping at Fredericksburg to say goodbye to his mother, he found and hired a man who said he could speak French.

Losing no time, they set out for the Blue Ridge Mountains and, in ten days, were as far into the woods as George had ever gone. From there on, he needed a guide. At a small settlement, he found a very shrewd one, Christopher Gist, and hired four woodsmen, two of whom spoke the Indian languages. With these guides, they set out for the village of Half King, a famous Indian chief, on the Ohio River. On the way, they learned that three Indian tribes had gone over to the French. What about Half King, was the question. Would they find him friendly or not?

Before finding out, they came to a point, not far from the Indian village, where two rivers joined to form the Ohio. George looked it over most carefully. On this point of land (where the city of Pittsburgh would be in years to come), was where the Ohio Company of Virginia planned to build their fort.

Half King was full of anger at the Frenchmen. This land, he said, was *his*. Frenchmen told him it was *theirs*. That was a bad lie. This was NO white man's land. This was *Indian* land!

George listened gravely, picked his words cautiously and waited—waited until Half King and three of his braves saw fit to guide them to the French fort.

They trailed after the Indians four days. Then they came upon a log trading post, flying the beautiful white flag of the French, with its golden lilies. A man half French, half Indian, was in charge. The fort, he said, was fifty miles farther on. But, he added, if the Englishman think the Frenchman would leave these lands, he is mistaken. Non! It belong to them. All these Ohio—all these Mississippi valley. LaSalle, a Frenchman discover it, many years ago. So would his commander tell them!

The French commander received Le Major Wash-eentong at his fort in a perfect manner. He took the Governor's courteous letter, asking him to leave, and wrote an equally courteous letter, saying NO.

Taking that letter back was one long struggle against the bitter cold. For now it was December. The ground was covered with snow. The horses were exhausted. In order to go faster, Washington (now in a suit of buckskin) proposed that he and Gist strap what they needed to their backs and trudge on ahead. Twice they came close to death. Trying to cross a half frozen river, George was hurled from their raft of logs and nearly drowned. Both were shot at by an Indian guide. But they plodded on.

And on January 16th, to the Governor's surprise and delight, Washington was back in Williamsburg. He had a report of the Ohio country, a drawing of the French fort and the French commander's letter.

In the Spring, on his second trip to the Ohio country, Washington was less successful. This time, upon the Governor's order, he took a company of soldiers, not a letter. During the past months, the Virginians had begun, at last, to build their fort at that point of land near the village of Half King. But even before the bright, new logs were all in place, the French had captured the fort. Now they had to be driven out!

Half way there, in a Great Meadow, surrounded by hills, Washington pitched his camp. He also built a temporary fort, though that low, open meadow was a foolish place to choose. But George had no training as a soldier. He had to learn from his mistakes.

One rainy night in May, an Indian runner came speeding into camp, with a message from Half King.

"French men nearby" said the Indian. "Half King see foot tracks. Thirty Frenchmen–maybe more."

Spies! thought Washington. The French were planning a surprise attack! There was no time to lose. He took forty men. All night they followed the Indian through the rain soaked woods. Half King joined them. About sunrise, the Indian stopped and pointed. There in a hollow were the Frenchmen!

An order was given to fire. For the first time, Washington heard bullets go whistling past his ears as the Frenchmen sprang to their guns. But too late. Their leader and ten of the men were dead. The other twenty were captured. Washington was overjoyed.

The first battle of his life had been a victory!

But his joy did not last long. On the third of July, five hundred furious Frenchmen, with many Indian allies came to attack him and avenge the "murder" of their comrades. Those men, they said, were only carrying a message to the English Governor.

It was a rainy, dismal day—the day of the battle. Inside his poor, little, unprotected fort in the Great Meadows, Washington had less than half as many men and had been deserted by Half King and his Indians. No wish to be captured in that white man's fort, Half King went to watch the battle from the hills.

Washington's men held out as long and bravely as they could, but by nightfall, he was obliged to surrender. In the light of a candle flickering in the wind, his translator read the French paper given him to sign. It said that he must give back the French prisoners and not return to that territory for another year. Washington signed it grimly. Next day, he was allowed to march his soldiers out of the fort with the honors of war, but he went home to Virginia, all his joy blotted out by this defeat.

To add to his misery, he fell ill and lay in bed for long, gloomy weeks, at Mount Vernon.

Meanwhile, copies of the paper he had signed reached England, and the King concluded it was time to send soldiers to America to settle what seemed to be turning into war against the French and Indians.

By the following summer, General Braddock had

arrived from England, and was in command. Washington, serving under him, was on another trip to recapture the log fort on the Ohio. Too ill, at times, to sit on a horse, he lay on his back in a baggage wagon. Bumping along, he kept fretting over the time wasted by the English General.

General Braddock was an old, experienced commander but he and his well trained soldiers had fought their battles in Europe, never in the wilderness. They had never heard wild Indian war whoops, nor known how a stealthy Indian crept up on a foe.

A first, horrible lesson came one day in July. In their brilliant scarlet coats, they were marching along through a narrow road in the forest, not far from the fort. Suddenly they heard a wild yell, and bullets whizzing from all directions. Soon they were falling dead and wounded. Yet they saw no enemy! Panic and frenzy swept their broken ranks. Into that stampede of men, rode General Braddock, on a rearing horse swinging his sword, shouting, trying to control his frantic soldiers. Washington, too, though still dizzy with fever, rode into the thick of the danger. Bullets whizzed by, pierced his sleeves, killed his horse. He mounted another. Wheeling here and there, he rallied his Virginians.

But the day was lost. General Braddock, himself, was wounded. Washington helped carry him from the field in a litter made of his scarlet sash. A few days later, they buried him there in the road, where his grave would be hidden from Indian scalp hunters under the tracks of his returning baggage wagons.

Two years later, in 1758, Washington made one last trip with the English soldiers to the Ohio fort. At their approach, the French hastily set fire to the fort and left. So Washington saw it go up at last in crackling flames, that little log fort in the wilderness, that had started the French and Indian War.

The French were to lose all of their forts and land in North America, by the time the war was over. Washington was to take no further part in it, but he had made a name for himself. At a meeting in Williamsburg, the chairman called attention to him.

"I wish to compliment our Virginia hero" said he "for his brave and steady behaviour from the first war-like actions of the French and their Indians to the capture of their fort."

Washington tried to reply, but no words came.

"Sit down, Mr. Washington" said the speaker, to relieve him. "Your modesty is equal to your bravery and that exceeds the power of any language I possess."

GEORGE AND MARTHA

ALONG the road, through pale yellow green of a soft spring day, came a fine travelling coach, topped by a coachman in braided livery, drawn by a team of sleek, high-stepping horses. Turning into the gate, it rolled up the lane and came to a stop in front of Mount Vernon. The footman jumped down, the coach door opened and out stepped George Washington.

Turning, he lifted out a tiny girl in a round hat with a feather on it, waited patiently for a small boy to clamber down by himself, and then gave his hand to the most important passenger–his wife!

A small pointed slipper appeared, a rustling brown skirt, the shirred top of a taffeta bonnet. Then she stood beside him, a plump little person barely up to her husband's shoulder. With a quick little gasp of pleasure, she looked up at the house.

"So this" she said "is Mount Vernon!"

There they were, George Washington and his new family–Patsy and Jacky and their mother, who had been Mrs. Martha Custis, the wealthiest young widow in the colony, until the 6th of January 1759. Then she had become Martha Washington. After their wedding, which had been a fashionable affair, they had gone to Williamsburg for the remainder of the winter. There they had enjoyed all the many amusements to be found in that gay, little capital of the colony.

Now it was Spring, and they were home. The door was wide open, a circle of house servants waiting just inside to welcome the new mistress. All was in readiness. Martha went from room to room, expressing her pleasure. At the same time, she quietly noted touches, here and there, that could be added.

George believed the mantel in the west parlor would be more elegant with the landscape and the bust of Julius Caesar he had ordered from England.

Upstairs, the bed rooms still smelled of new wall paper and freshly painted wood, for the ceilings had been raised and another half story added. Colonel George Fairfax, who lived nearby, George told her, had looked after the remodeling while he was away. From the east windows, they looked out over the Potomac. Near the landing they could see a man in a boat fishing for oysters. Downstairs then, they went, for dinner was served, after which, Jacky begged his wonderful new stepfather to show him again how he could crack nuts with his fingers!

Outside to be seen, were the kitchen, the spinning

HOME at

UNT VERNON

house and the servants' quarters. Martha went to sleep that night in the high four poster bed, feeling very much at home. Next day with needlework in hand, and her trunks unpacked, it seemed as if she had lived at Mount Vernon always.

Washington was to spend a busy summer. He was now learning to be a farmer. He loved the land and the cultivation of it—the very smell and feel of it. He enjoyed the rich, black furrows of earth following the plow—the even rows of young tobacco plants—long, brown leaves drying in the sheds—yellow mounds of hay and broad, rich fields of grain, replacing scrubby patches of woodland.

Whatever he undertook, he wanted to do well. So it was with farming. He tried to discover the crops best suited to the land, the best way to make them grow. He kept exact accounts and a careful record of everything. Nothing he did was slipshod.

Each night, while Martha was toeing off a sock or finishing a row of cross-stitch, George would sit down by a candle and write in his diary how he had spent the day, and whether it had been cloudy or fair.

One evening, he returned from another plantation to find Martha broken out with the measles. A few days later, he wrote that Sally Fairfax came to visit her. The evening being cold and the wind high, they sent their guest home in the chariot. Sunday morning it did not return in time, so they were prevented from going to church in Alexandria. But the next day, he rode to Alexandria to see about engaging a gardener and ordering a keg of butter. One evening they went there to attend a Ball, where "Musick" and dancing were the entertainment. He went fox hunting and duck hunting and fished for herring when they were in season. With Peter, the blacksmith, he tried to make a plow after a model he had designed. Eight new puppies were born, and he named them and greased them all with lard, when they had the mange. He sent apples to the cider mill and lumber to the saw mill. He found a Negro ill and brought him home for better care. He visited his mother and sister in Fredericksburg, and at various times helped his brothers Sam, Jack, and Charlie. He planted pine trees in the spring, and grafted peach and cherry trees, and tried out a machine for planting oats and barley. He and Martha dined with George and Sally Fairfax, and they, in turn, dined at Mount Vernon.

And so, pleasantly and happily the days and the seasons and the years passed by—fifteen peaceful years, until trouble from outside broke in upon them.

LOYAL SUBJECTS AND GEORGE III

THE STORY of that trouble goes back to a November evening in 1760, the year after George and Martha Washington were married. Williamsburg, always gay with theatre parties, card games and dancing was gayer than usual that November evening. For word had just been received that there was a new king! Young George III was now King of England.

"Long live the King!" cried the loyal Virginia planters, dining and dancing in the Raleigh Tavern.

"Long live the new King!" cried the royal Governor and his guests, dining in the "Palace."

In all the houses along the wide street, from the Capitol to the College, loyal subjects were drinking a health to their new King, George III.

George Washington was in Williamsburg with Martha and the children. He had come to attend the meeting of the legislature. This year, for the first time, he had been elected to the House of Burgesses.

Now the Governor of Virginia was appointed by the King. But members of the House of Burgesses were elected by the people. And they made the laws governing the colony. So, at least, it had always been.

But their new King, George III, had new ideas. It was not long before strange, new laws were being sent out from England, for governing the colonies! Every year these laws became more and more irritating, until one was finally passed called the Stamp Act. This brought on a hot discussion one May morning in the House of Burgesses. George Washington was in his seat as usual, when the Chairman called upon a new member, Mr. Patrick Henry.

Beyond the center table, draped in bright green felt, Washington saw a tall, angular man, wearing a coal-black wig, draw himself slowly to his feet, shove up his spectacles, and begin to speak.

"According to our rights as Englishmen," began Patrick Henry in a slow drawl, "We, the people of this colony are not obliged to obey the Stamp Act, nor" he paused, "any other such law not voted upon by this assembly." Speaking more rapidly, his voice, clear and ringing, rose in excitement. He called to mind other rulers, who, like George III, had been too eager for power, and therefore, had lost their lives . . . "And George III. . . . " said he.

"Treason!" shouted a man near Washington, jumping to his feet. "Treason!" shouted others, equally hasty and excitable. Washington, using better judgment, gave the speaker a fair chance to finish his sentence. It ended with the simple warning that George III had better learn from their example.

He then proposed a resolution that, as loyal subjects, they send a letter to His Majesty, the King, protesting against the Stamp Act. This seemed to them a reasonable action, but the royal Governor considered it an act of rebellion. He had the Burgesses dismissed, and locked out of the Capitol.

So much commotion was caused by the Stamp Act in every one of the colonies, that it had to be repealed, but then another law was passed. According to that law, Virginia planters were obliged to pay a tax on many of those things which they had always bought in England, in exchange for their tobacco. There was a tax to pay on glass, on paints, on china dishes, on building materials—even a tax on tea!

Members of the House of Burgesses, now locked out of the Capitol, gathered in the Raleigh Tavern to decide what to do. George Washington had a paper in his hand, as the meeting opened.

"I have a letter from Philadelphia," he said. "The people there have signed an agreement to buy none of those articles on which there is a tax, until that tax is removed. I propose that we, here in Virginia follow their most excellent example and refuse to buy."

So it was agreed, and soon from Massachusetts and other colonies, came word that their people also had similar agreements. What would happen next?

A frosty winter day in 1772 brought one answer to that question. That day, a post rider came galloping up to the Raleigh Tavern with startling news from Boston. Three shiploads of tea had arrived in Boston harbor. Rather than let the tea be unloaded and have to pay a tax on it, a party of men, dressed as Indians, had gone aboard and dumped it in the water. Following soon, came word that, in punishment, the harbor of Boston was to be closed and British soldiers sent there to enforce the King's command. That meant suffering for the people of Boston.

George Washington stood up–ready for action. "I am willing to raise a thousand men" he said "at my own expense and march to the relief of Boston."

A young lawyer, Thomas Jefferson, suggested that the day the port of Boston was closed should be observed in Williamsburg with prayer and fasting.

It was then June, 1774. For many months, the colonies had been keeping in touch with one another by mail. Now it seemed necessary for men from the various colonies to meet and talk together. So plans were made for a meeting to be held in Philadelphia. It was to be the First Continental Congress.

Seven delegates were chosen to represent Virginia. One was Patrick Henry, their famous orator, another was George Washington, still almost unknown outside of his own colony.

"But for solid judgment and information" said Patrick Henry, "I believe there will be no one to equal him at Philadelphia."

The September night before they left, Patrick Henry and one of the other delegates spent with Washington at Mount Vernon. Next afternoon, as they were finishing an early dinner, they heard the saddle horses being led up the driveway to the door.

"I do hope you will take a firm stand in the meeting" said Martha to the two guests as they were leaving. "I'm sure George will" she added, looking up at the big man and holding onto the lapels of his traveling coat, as he bent to say goodbye.

Jacky Custis, with his young bride, was standing beside his mother as the three men mounted their horses and, followed by servants in scarlet livery, cantered briskly off toward the main road.

Over fifteen years had now passed, since George Washington had first brought Martha and her two little children to Mount Vernon. Patsy had died the summer before. He was glad, now, not to be leaving Martha alone. Far down the road, he turned to look back at her and raised his hat; she waved her handkerchief and stood watching until he disappeared. They would have four days' journey to Philadelphia.

On horseback, in stagecoaches, all along the dusty roads leading to Philadelphia, in those early days of September 1774, came delegates to the First Continental Congress. Fifty-one of them—in their knee breeches and three-cornered hats—they came from all the colonies except Georgia, which had not received word in time. All were curious, as they unpacked their bags in the inns and taverns, to see what the strangers from other colonies were like.

George Washington was especially anxious to see the gentlemen from Boston, Samuel Adams and his cousin John Adams. There was a rumor that they were no longer loyal to the King—that they wanted to be FREE FROM ENGLAND! He couldn't believe it was possible, but he wanted to make sure. So, on the evening of September 28th, he walked over to talk with John Adams in his lodging house. It was his first chance to do so though for three weeks the two men had seen each other every day at the meetings of Congress. At least, Washington had seen the short stout little lawyer from Massachusetts, with his head of curly hair, bustling about among the delegates. But if John Adams had seen the big, silent, sunburned Virginia planter, he paid him no attention, not until he knocked on the door that evening, and entered the low second story room.

They talked of many things, but not once did either John Adams or cousin Sam even mention the words "freedom" or "independence." Washington felt sure they did not want it, but he was wrong.

The truth was, that they had been warned ahead of time. Five miles outside of Philadelphia, in their stagecoach, they had been met by friends, who had gone out to warn them to be on their guard.

"Philadelphia is full of Loyalists" they said "to them and to the Virginia delegates the very word INDEPENDENCE would be shocking." So, neither that night, nor at any meeting of the Congress, was there a word said about separating from the mother country. The delegates merely drew up a petition to the King, in which, as "his Majesty's faithful subjects" they begged their "Most Gracious Sovereign" for justice. Then they went home, planning to meet again in May, when they hoped to have an answer from the king.

The winter passed and there was no answer. March came, with cherry trees blossoming at Mount Vernon. And still no answer from the King.

"It is useless to wait longer" said Patrick Henry, in a Virginia meeting, which Washington attended. "The time for action is at hand. We must fight for our rights. I know not what course others may take—but as for me—Give me LIBERTY, or give me death!"

Believing that they must fight, the people of Virginia began drilling and arming companies of soldiers. They asked Washington to take command. So it was not as a planter, but as a soldier, wearing his military uniform of blue and tan, that George Washington set out for the second time, for Congress in Philadelphia. It would be many years before he would be home again, for the quiet years at Mount Vernon were over.

It was May 1775. And now, when George Washington was forty-three years old, that part of his life that was to test his character and measure his greatness was about to begin.

one cold winter was spent
at Valley Forge
the French came to help America
the British surrendered at Yorktown, Virginia
1781

The first shots were fired
the day after Paul Revere's ride
by Minute Men of Massachusetts
The Declaration of Independence
this is Independence
Christmas night 1776 Wash
the Delaware
WAR OF 1776

GENERAL WASHINGTON

JOHN ADAMS saw him at once. The minute George Washington entered the State House at Philadelphia he caught sight of the military uniform.

"There" said he "is one man, ready for action."

John Adams had come down from Boston, hoping to find all the delegates to this Second Congress as ready for war, as the ones from Massachusetts.

Certainly they should be, for war *had actually begun!* Two weeks before, on an April night, Paul Revere had made his wild ride from Boston to warn the people of Concord that the "Red-Coats" were coming. The next morning, April 19th, the first shots had been fired between the "Minute Men" of Massachusetts and the British soldiers. The first battle in the American Revolution had been fought.

And yet, to his disgust, John Adams found the delegates still divided and wavering and wondering what to do. By the middle of June, he was snorting with indignation. Out for a breath of air in the yard of the State House, he made up his mind to act. Accordingly, when Congress had reassembled, he rose briskly, made a short speech, and then said,

"I move that Congress should adopt the army (near Boston) and appoint a General. I have but one gentleman in mind for that important command. That is a gentleman from Virginia, whose independent fortune and great talents and excellent character would unite the colonies better than any other person in the whole thirteen."

A few days later, Washington was unanimously elected, and on June 16th, John Hancock, President of the Congress informed Mr. Washington that he had been chosen Commander-in-Chief of the Army.

"Mr. President" said Washington, slowly, as he rose to his feet. "Although I am truly sensible of the high honor, I declare with utmost sincerity, I do not think myself equal to the command. As to pay, sir, I do not wish any. I will keep an exact account of my expenses and that is all that I desire."

Just one week later, the new General left for Boston. On July 3, 1775, General Washington reached Cambridge, just across the river. There he saw, for the first time, the odd assortment of half-trained troops, independent farmer boys, lanky backwoodsmen gathered into this willing, but peculiar army. This was the army with which he was now supposed to drive the well trained British soldiers out of Boston.

THE WAR FOR INDEPENDENCE

ON JULY 4, 1776, the United States was born. Exactly one year after Washington took command of the army, the colonies declared themselves free from England. Their Declaration of Independence had been written by Thomas Jefferson and signed.

George Washington did not sign it. On that day in July, when it was first read aloud to the members of Congress in Philadelphia, he was in New York City with his army. There, as soon as a copy came, he had it read aloud to the men. The soldiers, excited to hear that they were no longer subjects of George III, ran to the park, tore down his statue, knocked off his head and melted his lead horse into bullets.

George Washington did not approve of such disrespectful conduct, but he did approve of Independence. More than any one else, he was to make that Declaration, now only written on paper, become true. He believed that the colonies should be free and was willing to fight for their freedom.

And a long hard fight it was to be. Six years would pass from the time the first shots had been fired in Massachusetts until all firing ended at Yorktown, in

Virginia; and two more years before the treaty was signed and the war was actually over.

Eight long discouraging years those would be for Washington. He had to carry on a war, when he had nothing to fight with—never enough soldiers—not enough guns and ammunition for those he did have—not enough clothes—not even enough food. And no pay for them, for Congress had no money.

Yet Congress would order him to do impossible things and blame him when he failed. Some of his officers were to lose faith in him, and form a plot to ruin him. One of those he most trusted was to turn traitor. Still he would keep steadily on through those eight years, doing the best he could with what he had and holding on—holding on.

Now the first year was over. The winter had been spent on the hills outside of Boston. In the Spring, the British had decided to leave the harbor. Through his spy glass, Washington had watched them as they boarded their ships and sailed away.

Following orders from Congress, Washington had then moved his patchwork army down to New York to try to keep that city from being captured next. But it proved impossible. For one thing, he had no war-ships to keep the British ships from entering the harbor. So General Howe sailed in. Having almost twice as many men, he defeated the Americans, drove them out of the city, chased them up the Hudson River, and across the river into New Jersey. That was enough for him. He went back to New York.

There he found Lord Cornwallis, who had just arrived from England, bringing Hessian soldiers, who had been hired to fight. So Howe sent them to carry on the chase. Week after week it went on. Month after month, down through New Jersey, Washington kept on retreating, with the enemy close upon his heels, like a pack of hounds chasing a fox.

Moving too fast to carry supplies, his cold, hungry troops began deserting. Some of his officers now turned against him. And when he had to cross the Delaware River into Pennsylvania, Congress was in a panic. Any day they expected to see Cornwallis and his soldiers come marching into Philadelphia.

But it was then December. The Delaware River was too difficult to cross, half frozen, full of floating ice cakes. So the soldiers, whom Cornwallis had sent on ahead of him, stopped short on the Jersey side in the town of Trenton. Christmas came. Feasting, drinking, singing songs of their homeland, the Hessians celebrated all day and far into the night.

During that night Washington re-crossed the Delaware. In the blinding snow and sleet, in small boats, he brought his men back across that half frozen river to the New Jersey side. At dawn, they rushed in upon the sleepy, groggy soldiers and captured them. Washington was still there, when Cornwallis arrived.

"I'll bag the old fox now" said Cornwallis, that night, planning to capture Washington in the morning. But next morning he awoke to find that his "old fox" had been too sly for him. He had escaped!

While Cornwallis slept, Washington had slipped away in the dark. Leaving his campfires burning to fool the British sentinels into thinking he was still there, he had stolen silently around the enemy lines. By daylight, he and his soldiers were well away and on the road north again. A battle at Princeton, in which the British were defeated, ended the fighting for that winter. Cornwallis returned to New York. Washington went into winter camp in New Jersey. Martha came from Mount Vernon to be with him, and kept busy knitting stockings. She left in early summer when the fighting was expected to begin again.

Just where it would begin, or what city the British would try to capture next, Washington could only guess—until about the first of August.

Then his scouts brought word that General Howe had sailed from New York harbor. Two weeks later, British ships were seen sailing into Chesapeake Bay. No doubt then. They were headed for Philadelphia!

Congress scurried away, and the "rebels" left in Philadelphia were terrified. Hoping to give them courage, Washington marched his soldiers through the streets and down past the Hall where the bold Declaration of Independence had so recently been signed. To the tune of "Yankee Doodle" on their fife and drums, the men and boys stepped along as briskly and bravely as they could, behind their devoted leader. Sprigs of green leaves were stuck in their ragged caps, to make them look a trifle less dilapidated.

Cheered by the rebels, the ragged troops were jeered and laughed at by the Tories. And there were many of them—many of those Americans who were still loyal to the King. They longed to hear and see the British entering their city. A battle or two, and they were there. Early in October, General Howe and his soldiers were marching into Philadelphia. The city was all theirs for a gay and comfortable winter.

Only twenty miles away, Washington and his soldiers suffered through the winter on the bleak, windswept hills at Valley Forge, half starved, half frozen.

Many had no shoes, and their sore, cracked feet, wrapped in rags, left tracks of blood in the snow as they went about cutting down trees and building log huts to live in. Until the huts were finished, Washington stayed in a tent close to his men, and lived and ate as they did. Then he moved into a small stone house, down by the creek. Martha came, as usual, to spend the winter months. Bright days she trudged from hut to hut, with a basket on her arm, visiting soldiers who were ill. Every day but Sunday she was knitting socks and patching garments with wives of the other officers.

Washington lived through that winter with a heavy heart. He was distressed by the suffering of his soldiers. He was tormented by letters from Congress filled with blame and criticism, and offering no help. He discovered that a plot was being formed to ruin him and put another general in his place. Hurt by their lack of trust, Washington still kept up his courage, stood firm and held on. In time the cruel plot against him melted away and also that dreadful winter came to an end.

And it was Spring again—the Spring of 1778.

And with that Spring came news—GOOD news—GREAT news! WONDERFUL NEWS!

One day in May, the whole camp was given over to celebration and joy. So overjoyed was one young Major General, that he threw his arms around Washington and kissed him on both cheeks! This was the Marquis de La Fayette, a young French nobleman, just twenty years old. And the cause of his great joy?

France, his country—*France had now joined America in the war!* A treaty had just been signed by Louis XVI, the King of France, and Benjamin Franklin, who had gone there to ask France for help.

Only a year ago he, La Fayette, had left for America to help fight for Liberty. Then he had had to slip away to the seaport in disguise, with a black wig over his red hair, because the King had forbidden him to leave. Now the King had changed his mind. France was going to help America. French soldiers and French ships would soon be coming!

That news changed the plans of the British. General Howe had now returned to England, leaving another general in command. Hearing that a French fleet was sailing for New York, the British general felt he was needed there more than in Philadelphia. So he left, and, dragging after him a train of baggage wagons twelve miles long, returned to New York City. Washington followed, and went into camp not far off, where he could keep watch of the city and wait for the French fleet. As soon as the French ships came, Washington hoped, with their help, to recapture the city and drive the British from New York.

What a disappointment! The French ships got there in July, but their hulls were so deep that they dragged in the sand bar, got stuck and couldn't even enter the harbor. So the British stayed in New York and Washington and his troops stood guard nearby, to the end of the war.

And from then on to the end, most of the fighting was in the four southern states. It began in Georgia. By the Spring of 1780, the fifth year of the war, the British had marched up through Georgia, through South Carolina, and Lord Cornwallis, who was in command, had moved on into North Carolina, headed for Virginia. That was sad news for Washington, but there was also good news.

French soldiers had landed in America, and were in Newport, Rhode Island. Taking La Fayette with him, Washington went to confer with the friendly, old French general, whom his soldiers called "papa" Rochambeau. Again he was hoping to attack the British general in New York, but it seemed wiser not to try, until another French fleet reached America. Another was on its way. So there was nothing to do but wait, while that fifth year dragged slowly out. Early the next year, 1781, Washington heard from Thomas Jefferson, who was then governor of Virginia, that British troops were marching through Virginia, burning tobacco warehouses, and laying waste to the country. Washington sent La Fayette south at once, with all the soldiers he could possibly spare.

Soon he heard that Cornwallis was also in Virginia. He waited anxiously for La Fayette's letters.

At last, in early autumn, word came to hurry south as fast as possible.

The French fleet had arrived in Chesapeake Bay! The American generals had Cornwallis surrounded and he was bottled up in Yorktown.

Washington and Rochambeau started south at once. Soon the ragged American soldiers and the French troops, in their gorgeous uniforms, cheered by the people, were marching through Philadelphia, through Baltimore, and crossing the Potomac into Virginia. Late one night, the family at Mount Vernon were startled out of their sleep. There, to their surprise was Washington, himself! The next day, came "papa" Rochambeau. A fine feast was given them by the neighbors. And they were off again.

Jacky Custis went as an aide to Washington, saying what was to be a last goodbye to his three little girls and baby son. He would not return.

At Williamsburg, ten miles from Yorktown, Washington found La Fayette waiting, overjoyed to see his great and beloved general there at last.

On October 9, 1781, the siege of Yorktown began. Washington touched off the first cannon. For ten days the cannons boomed and clouds of smoke hung over the little town. Then the firing ceased.

Cornwallis surrendered.

At two o'clock in the afternoon, with the bright October sun shining on their scarlet coats, the British soldiers marched slowly out of Yorktown, while their band played a popular British tune, "The World Upside Down". They passed between rows of French and American soldiers drawn up in parallel lines. The troops stood in respectful silence, as Washington had told them to do, while the British soldiers laid down their arms.

The day after the surrender Cornwallis went to pay his respects to General Washington. And, shortly afterward, he was a guest at the dinner that Washington gave for the officers of the three armies.

Jacky Custis now lay desperately ill in Williamsburg. His wife and mother hurried from Mount Vernon. And just before he died, Washington promised to adopt his littlest girl, Nelly, who was two and a half and his baby boy, named George Washington.

So Cornwallis had surrendered. Almost everyone thought the war was over. But, not until the British left New York, and not until the peace treaty had actually been signed by the ministers of George III, would the war be over. So the American soldiers could not be discharged. It was almost more than Washington could do to hold the men together, they were so impatient and so restless. And so furious at not having been paid. They blamed Congress bitterly.

They even suggested that Washington should seize the power and run the country himself. He should overthrow the government and make himself KING!

Washington was shocked. Calling a meeting, he begged them to do nothing to "overturn the liberty of their country or spoil the glory they had won." And only because they so believed in him and trusted him, were they willing to follow him and remain loyal to the established government and Congress.

Two months after the treaty had been signed, the good word reached America, and in April 1783, the proclamation was read aloud to the soldiers. They were then discharged, and the British left the country.

On December 4, in New York City, at Fraunces Tavern, Washington met with his officers to bid them farewell. As he looked into their faces, he was unable to speak. Then he steadied himself.

"With a heart full of love and gratitude" he said, "I take my leave of you, most devoutly wishing that your latter days may be as prosperous and happy as your former ones have been glorious and honorable."

At his request, they passed by, one by one, and clasped his hand, without saying a word. Then they watched him walk to the shore where a barge was waiting. As it moved slowly away, they saw him stand gazing back at them, his hat held high in his hand.

Independence had been won.

Everywhere that Washington went now there were cheering crowds to welcome him. Balls and banquets were given in his honor. At Philadelphia, he stopped to give the Treasurer an exact account of his expenses. From there, he went to Annapolis, Maryland, where Congress was then meeting, and resigned his general's commission. And then, on Christmas Eve, with Martha sitting beside him in the coach, George Washington, after eight years of war, was riding home at last, to his peaceful, beloved Mount Vernon.

vegetable garden

stables

coaches

washing

to smoke meats

butler

kitchen

green house
flower garden
stores
spinning-weaving
tools
office
Plan of MOUNT VERNON

NELLY

CHRISTMAS EVE at Mount Vernon. The house was full of evergreen and holly. And Grandpapa was coming home! All afternoon little Nelly Custis had been waiting for him, in her white muslin dress and her new blue sash, very wide and floating for a five-year-old. All afternoon, she had been skipping to the window to see if his coach was coming up the drive. And her baby brother had been running after her and their mammy after him, to keep him from going outside in the cold. For the door kept opening, coaches driving up, guests coming in—but no grandpapa!

Nelly was certain she would recognize him. He was a very big soldier. Grandmother had told her all about him, and told the cook, too. She knew just what he liked to eat, and had good-smelling meats roasting in the kitchen and plum puddings boiling in a bag.

It was dusky outside now, and beginning to snow. Inside, Nelly watched the flames curl about the hickory logs and go blazing up the chimney. She picked up a mistletoe berry that had fallen off, and then she heard horses' hooves plopping in the driveway. She ran to the door. And THERE they WERE!

Grandmother's round cheeks were pink and cold, when she kissed them. There were bits of snow on Grandfather's eyelashes, and stars of it on his three-cornered hat, and on the shoulders of his long cape, lined with red. And his black boots were very shiny.

So were the boots of the French officers who followed him. More guests and more guests, they gathered round her grandfather so that she could hardly see him—not till after the Christmas holidays. Then it grew so cold, that nobody could come at all.

And then what fun they had, she and grandpapa together! He made drawings of the house, as it was going to be. On the side toward the river he drew a piazza with eight tall pillars, and on the roof, a cupola with a weather vane. On the other side, he marked out two new gardens and a lawn for bowling. Around that he made a curving line that was to be the driveway. And all over he put little dots to show where new trees were to be planted. And whenever Mammy told her not to be a bother, grandfather said,

"It's all right. Nelly is helping me."

So when Spring came, she went out to help put in the little trees and walked about and talked about lots of little things grandfather believed he never would have thought about if it hadn't been for Nelly!

MR. PRESIDENT

"PRESIDENT of the United States" George Washington's heart sank, when he first heard those words. It was April 14th, 1789. He had just come in from his morning ride over the plantation, and was standing in the dining room at Mount Vernon. There, with the family about him, he heard the messenger from Congress announce that he had been unanimously elected the first President of the United States. The FIRST President. What a difficult assignment! For months he had feared it would be his. Now he felt like a condemned man who had received his sentence.

Once he had set out upon an unknown journey into the northwest, but there had been a faint trail to follow. There had been guides. But on this journey, no one had ever gone ahead of him. There was no path, no guide to follow—nothing. There had never been a President of the United States before—nor had there been a truly UNITED States until after 1787.

All through the war, the thirteen colonies had been but loosely joined together, like so many little nations. They had begun to fall apart and quarrel with one another, as soon as the war was over and they were no longer held together by fear. With great dismay, Washington had seen this happen. So had other men all over the country, who had its welfare at heart.

In May, 1787, they had decided to meet together in Philadelphia, to see what could be done to make a firmer and more perfect union. The plans and regulations they worked out became the Constitution of the United States. It had taken four months for the delegates to agree, and a year for the plan to be approved by the various states. Then, in January, 1789, the people had voted for the electors, the electors had then voted for the President. In March, the new Congress had met in New York City. And now, in April, the elected president was leaving home.

He had asked that his entry into New York be kept very simple, but Congress had prepared an elaborate reception. A committee was sent to meet him across the harbor in New Jersey. From there a splendid barge, hung with flags, rowed by thirteen pilots in white uniforms, carried him across the water to the foot of Wall Street. Flags were flying, buildings festooned with flowers, streets lined with cheering people. The air was filled with the music of bands and the salute of cannon. That was his reception. His inauguration had to be delayed until Congress had finished arguing over the proper way to speak to him. "Your Royal Majesty" was the way to address a King. But what about a president? Should one say, "Your Serene Highness" or "Your High Mightiness" or what? Mr. James Madison, who had helped write the Constitution, finally settled it by saying he was to be called just Mr. President.

"To me, that sounds like the head of a fire company" remarked John Adams, seated under a red velvet canopy in front of the Senate. Having received the second largest vote, he was the Vice President.

On the balcony, outside of the Senate Chamber, the President was to take the oath of office, on April 30th, shortly after noon. A great crowd was gathered in the street below. As Washington stepped out and looked down upon their faces, he felt weak and ill. They expected too much of him—more than he was equal to. Then, gathering his courage he stepped forward, placed his hands on the Bible and took the vow:

"I do solemnly swear that I will faithfully execute the office of President of the United States and will to the best of my ability preserve, protect and defend the Constitution of the United States."

A cheer rose from the people. "God bless George Washington! Long live our President!"

Nelly loved being the granddaughter of the President and going to live in the big city of New York, where there were over 30,000 people! She liked hearing everyone call her grandmother Lady Washington. She liked seeing the fashionable ladies who came to the receptions and the way they wore their hair, powdered white and piled up and up and UP with ribbons and ostrich feathers on the top.

Grandmother gave a reception on their first Friday evening. Nelly and little "Washington" were allowed to come in for a while. Grandfather gave receptions on Tuesdays but they were only for gentlemen. He usually wore a black velvet suit and looked very handsome in it, with his hair powdered white. Sometimes he wore a brown suit, with gold buttons, which had an eagle on them, holding thirteen arrows.

But for a while he was ill, and there was a rope stretched across the street, so that no noisy carriages could go by their house. Nelly didn't even have to practice her spinet. But when he was well again, they all four went out riding in the coach, for long rides, almost every Saturday.

The next winter, Grandfather said, they would be in Philadelphia. The capital was going to be moved.

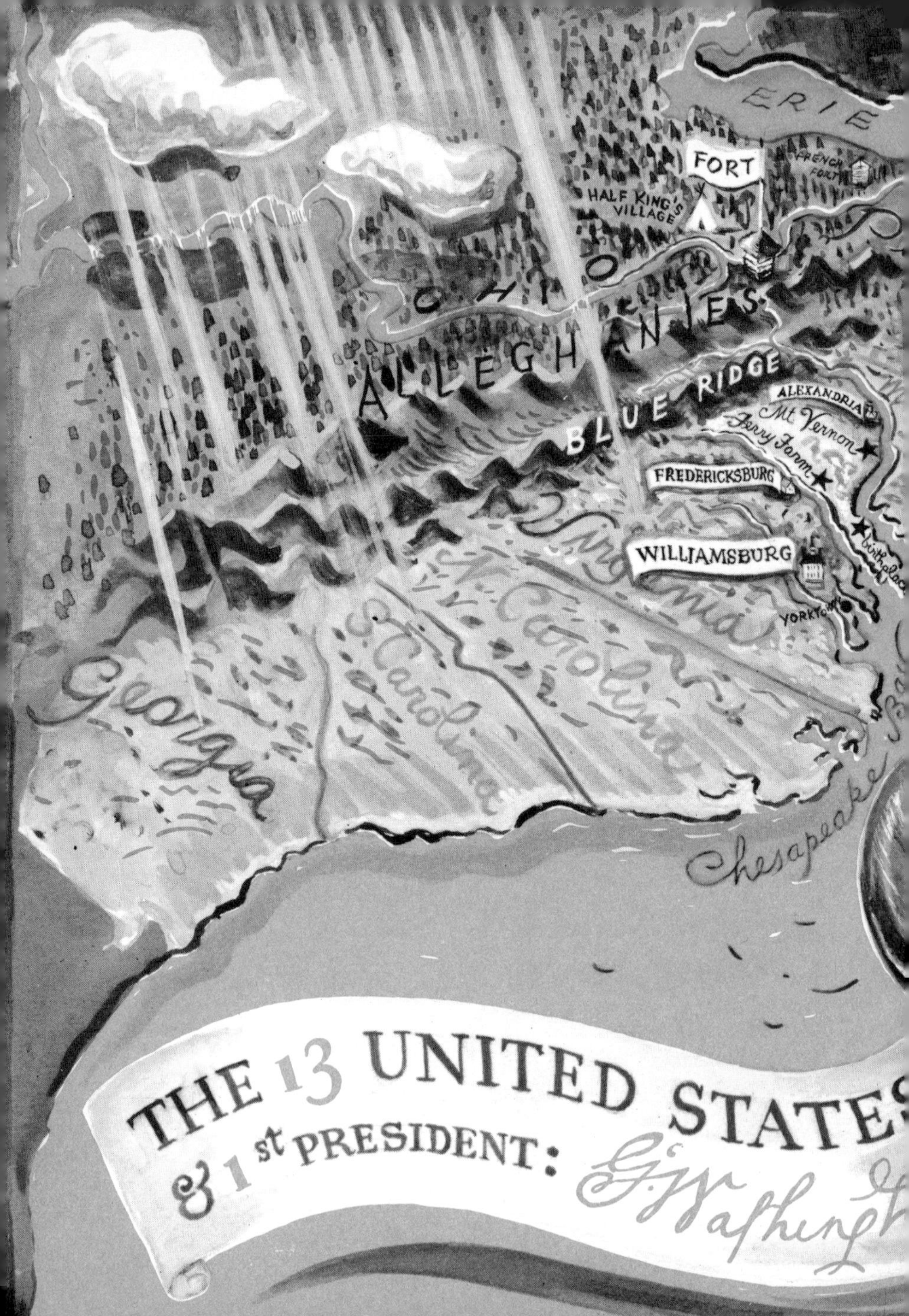
ERIE
FORT
FRENCH FORT
HALF KING'S VILLAGE
OHIO
ALLEGHANIES
BLUE RIDGE
ALEXANDRIA
Mt Vernon
Ferry Farm
FREDERICKSBURG
WILLIAMSBURG
YORKTOWN
Virginia
N. Carolina
S. Carolina
Georgia
Chesapeake
THE 13 UNITED STATES
& 1st PRESIDENT:

PHILADELPHIA
New York
BOSTON
New Hampshire
Massachusetts
Connecticut
R.I.
VALLEY FORGE
TRENTON
New Jersey
Hudson River
Delaware
Delaware River

THE NEW CAPITAL: WASHINGTON, D. C.

On some fields and woodlands across the Potomac River from Alexandria, surveyors were at work one day in June 1791. They were laying out a new city.

George Washington, in company with a younger man, was watching them from an old tobacco field, on top of a hill. A soft breeze was blowing and in the blue sky above them floated small puffy white clouds. On just such a perfect summer day, as this, forty-two years ago, Washington had been a young surveyor helping lay out the town of Alexandria. Now he was fifty-nine years old, President of the United States.

He had chosen this place across his beloved Potomac as a home for the new nation. Here a new capital city was being made to order. His companion, carrying a roll of drawings, was the French architect selected to design it. They had come this afternoon to choose sites for the principal buildings. On this hilltop, they agreed, should be built the House of Congress, with many streets radiating from it.

More than a year ago, Congress had decided, after wandering from city to city, that they must select a permanent home. But then they had had to argue loud and long before they could agree on where it should be located. Part of this now chosen land had been granted by Maryland. Part of it had to be purchased. At first, some of the owners asked such a high price, that Washington was obliged to come from Philadelphia, to reason with them.

"Remember" he said to one stubborn old Scotsman, "had it not been for the Federal City, you'd not have sold your land at all, and died a poor man."

"Aye, mon" retorted Mr. Burns, "an had ye not married the rich widow Custis, you'd a been a land surveyor to this day, and a poor one a'that!"

In the end, Mr. Burns (who happened to own the piece where they now planned to put the President's "Palace") and all the other owners were satisfied.

The surveyors had then cleared a strip around the entire tract of land, which was ten miles square, and set up stone posts a mile apart to show that it belonged to the United States. This was the District of Columbia, named by Thomas Jefferson, Madison and the committee who had purchased it. To the city, which they hoped to see built there in ten years, they had given the name of WASHINGTON. But Washington himself never used it. All of his life he simply and modestly called it the Federal City.

THE PRESIDENT KEEPS PEACE

GEORGE WASHINGTON'S first four years as President were quiet and easy compared to his second term. He had again received all of the electors' votes. Hardly, however, had the people shown their great trust in him, than many were saying that he didn't know his business—that he was ungrateful, unfaithful, dishonest, a fool, even a traitor! And why?

He refused to declare war.

This was the time of the great French Revolution. The French had beheaded their King, Louis XVI; were about to behead their Queen. They had done away with royalty, set up a Republic, and terrified all the other kings of Europe. So nearly every country, including England, had gone to war against France.

"Poor France" cried people in the United States. "France helped us fight our war. We must help her."

"That's ridiculous" said others, "It was their King Louis XVI who helped us, not this rabble of commoners who murdered him. We should help England punish France and restore law and order in Europe."

The United States was split into two parties. One party was clamoring for war against France, the other party was clamoring for war against England.

Crowds waving the new French flag went milling around Washington's house in Philadelphia, for several days, threatening to drag him out and force him to help the French Republic. Why not? Had he forgotten that the French had helped the colonies in America fight for their Republic?

No. Washington remembered very well the French soldiers standing with the Americans at Yorktown. He also remembered a battle in the wilderness when he had stood with the English, fighting against the French and Indians. He had fought both with France and against France, with England and against England; but right here in America, not in Europe. And right here Americans would still have enough to do protecting themselves and building up their country, without being drawn into another war.

What this country needed was peace in which to raise crops and build factories. Not war, but peace. So Washington had refused to declare war, and had brought upon himself this storm of abuse. He could bear it, for he knew that it was ill-founded and so would not last. But he was very tired, and at the end of his term, he was glad to turn over the office of President to his successor, John Adams.

Everyone's eyes were moist with tears, said John Adams, as they bade goodbye to their first President, on his last day in office. And everywhere along his journey home, Washington was met by cheering crowds and guards of honor and words of praise. It gave him great satisfaction, for he said later, "To have received the approval of my country, fulfills my greatest wish and all my ambition."

And now the beautiful cream-colored coach, drawn by eight horses, was turning into the gateway at Mount Vernon, and he was home again. And very happy, Nelly could see, to be once more "Farmer Washington." That summer, writing to a friend, the "happy farmer" said he began each day with the sun, walking about, looking over the various buildings until breakfast was ready (a little after seven). Then, he said "I mount my horse and ride round my farms (until) it is time to dress for dinner, at which I rarely miss seeing strange faces, come, as they say, out of respect for me. The usual time of sitting at table, a walk and tea bring me within the dawn of candlelight. I then resolve that I will retire to my writing table and acknowledge the letters I have received, but when the lights are brought, I feel tired. . . ."

Though too tired to write letters at night, he still

wrote in his diary, as he had always done. His last two birthdays were pleasant to record. In 1798, on his sixty-sixth, with Martha he attended his annual Birthday Ball in Alexandria. Though "their dancing days were over", it was a joy to watch his gay, pretty Nelly dancing the minuet with his favorite nephew, Lawrence Lewis, son of his sister Betty. In 1799, on February 22nd, about candlelight, Nelly came down the stairway at Mount Vernon in her wedding gown, to marry Lawrence Lewis. And late in November, Washington became greatgrandpapa to a baby girl.

Friday, December 13, 1799 was the last day of which he wrote. Thursday it had been snowing and when he came in for dinner, there was snow hanging on his hair, and his neck was wet. Saturday, he became very ill, and lived only a few hours more.

Death was not strange and troubling when it came to him, but quiet and restful, like sleep. He simply closed his eyes, and that part of life that he had known and lived so well was over.

By Christmas, the news that George Washington was gone, had spread in waves of sorrow to all parts of the nation, which he had led in war and in peace. He had won a lasting place of honor and affection in the hearts of his countrymen and in the world.

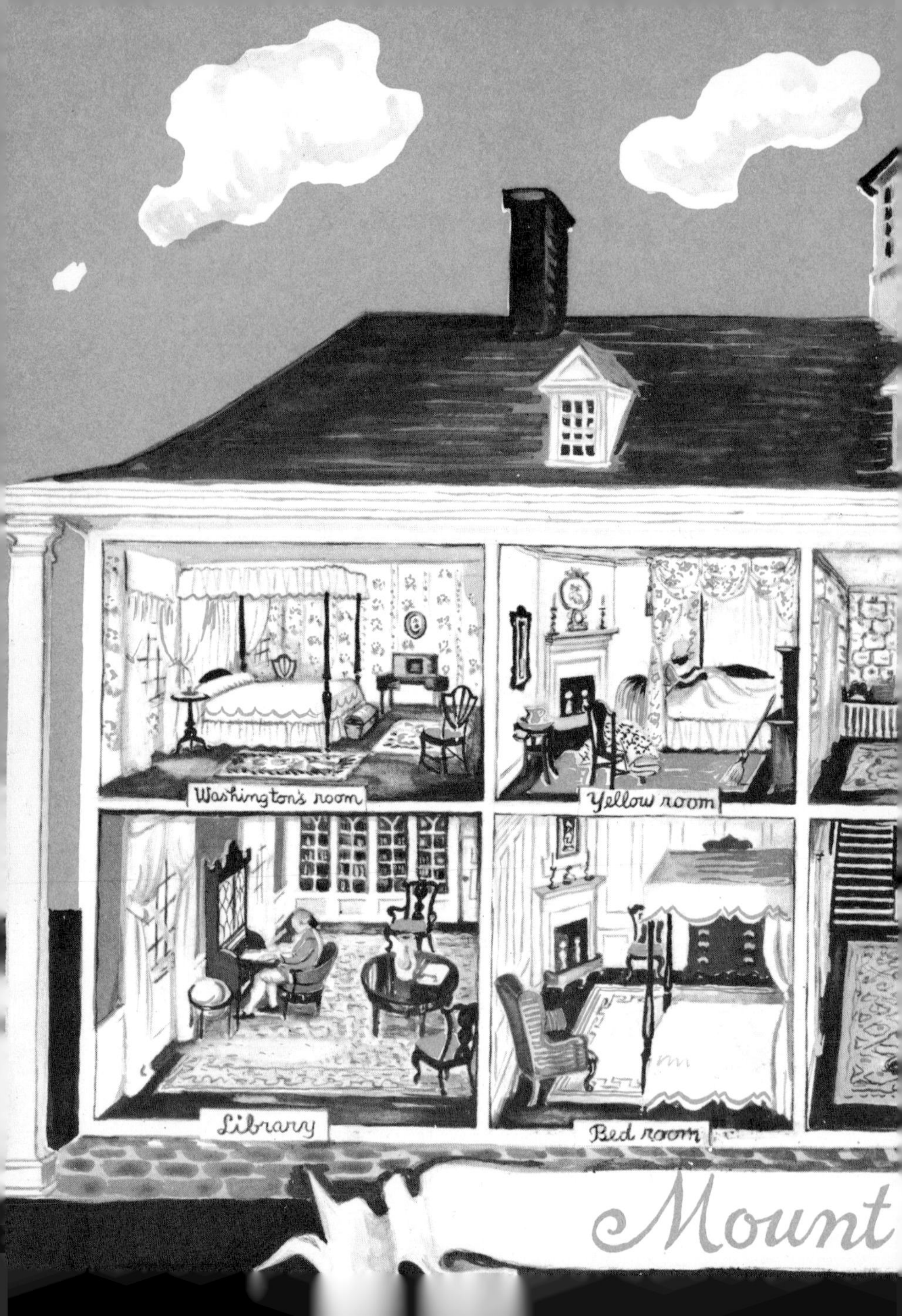
Washington's room
Yellow room
Library
Bed room
Mount

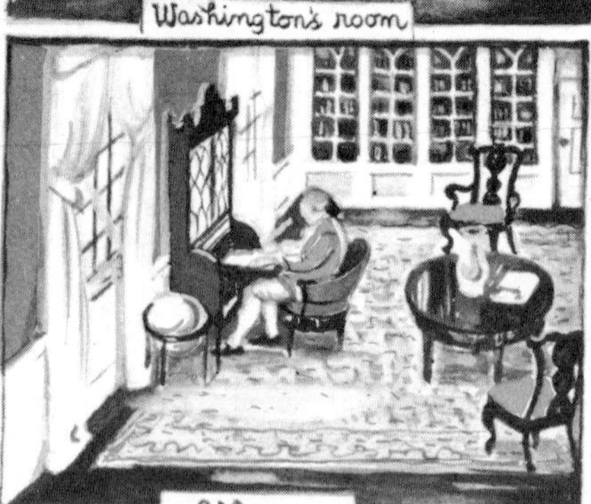

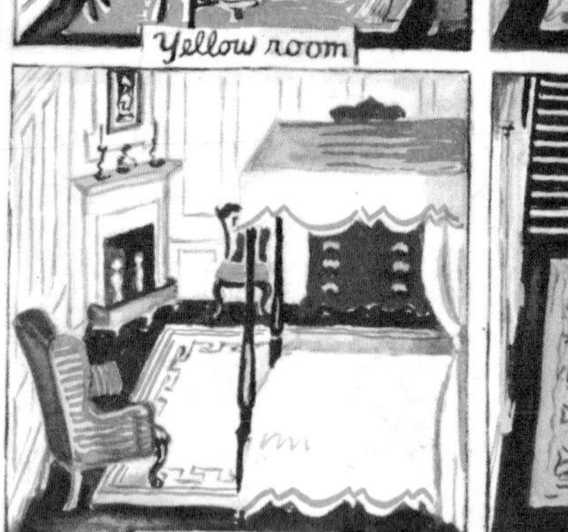

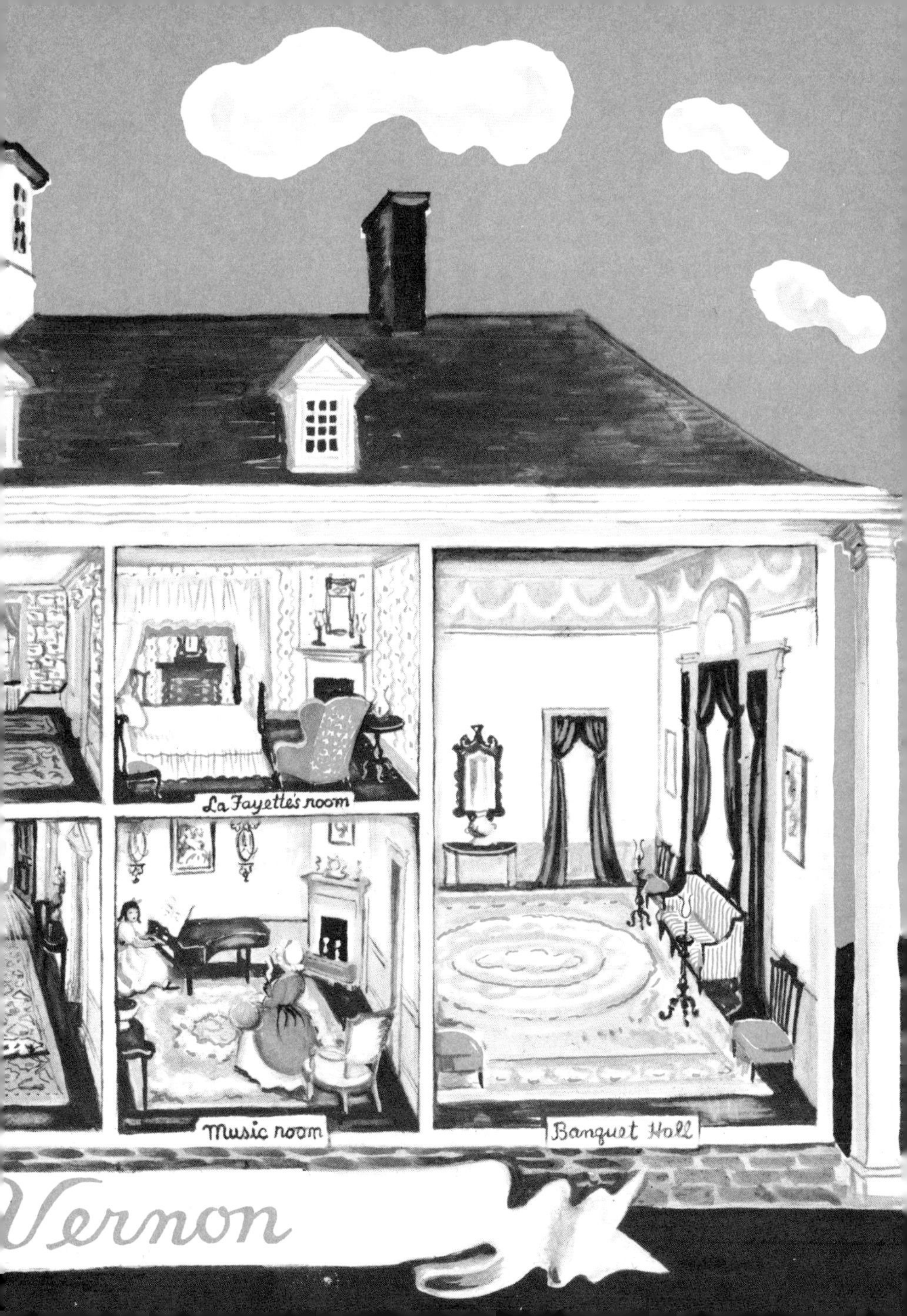
La Fayette's room
Music room
Banquet Hall
Vernon

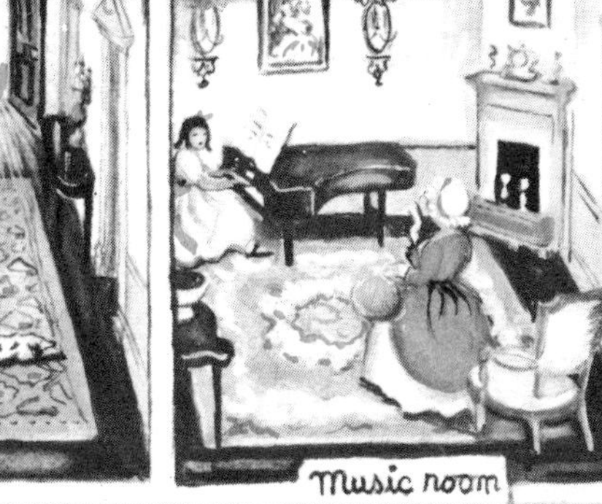

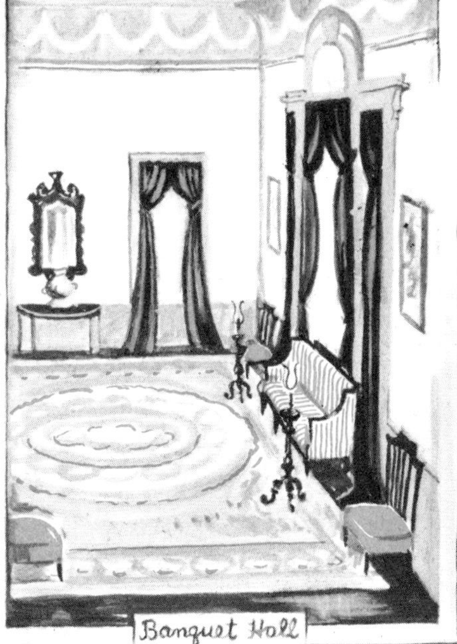

If you go to Mount Vernon you will see a small hall and a staircase connecting the library and George Washington's bedroom. These were left out of this drawing because it was so small.

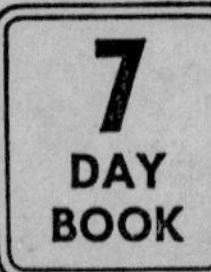

B
W
24,140

Foster, Genevieve (Stump)

George Washington